How to Grieve

EVEN WHEN YOU DON'T WANT TO

VALERIE IHSAN

WillowBenchBooks

How To Grieve: Even When You Don't Want To

Valerie Ihsan

How To Grieve: Even When You Don't Want To © 2014 Valerie Ihsan

All rights reserved. This book or any portion thereof may not be reproduced or used in any manner whatsoever without the express written permission of the publisher, except for the use of brief quotations in a book review.

Printed in the United States of America

Cover Design: paperandsage.com

Foreword

When I was 26, I told my husband, Rob, we were finally pregnant with our second child. We'd been trying for eight months. Later that same day, Rob died. He'd fallen asleep driving and hit a highway signpost.

I was pregnant and was now a widow. I had a 22-month-old daughter.

I didn't know how to be a widow. I didn't know any widows. I had no road map, no blueprints. There was no how-to guide—and prior to 9/11 there weren't many books on grieving a spouse at such a young age.

Let this booklet be that guide for you.

—Certified Bereavement Facilitator since 2004; Widow since 2000.

Afterwards

AFTER YOU'VE HEARD THE NEWS, EVERYTHING IS A normal reaction. You could cry, scream, stare at the wall, rock your- self, eat, or throw up. It's all normal. There's no one right way to grieve.

LET SOMEONE KNOW. Let your family/friends/neighbors help you. You can't do this alone. Most likely someone else will pick up the reins at this point and finish notifying whoever needs knowing. Food will materialize. Your house chores will start being done by others, and you can continue to stare at the wall. That's what I did. I cried, too, but mostly I just sat. And waited. For whatever was going to happen next.

MAKE ONLY IMMEDIATE DECISIONS. There'll be plenty of other little things you'll be called upon to deal with. Don't worry about the long-term stuff right now. The mainstream advice is not to make any major decisions right after a tragedy. Some- times it can't be helped—like approving an organ transplant, or needing to move out of the rental house that you can no longer afford on one salary—but put off whatever you can. I was fortunate enough to not have to decide anything at first, except choosing his casket and answering funeral/wake related questions.

Your head and heart are so full of other things, you aren't in your right mind. How can you make a major life decision at this time? I *did* move after my husband died, but I waited six months before deciding and then made it happen in the following two. Part of my hurry was my pregnancy. I wanted to be settled before I gave birth. But I still staged it so that there were built-in chunks of time where I could stop and reassess.

And I had family helping me through the process.

For instance, when I moved to Oregon, I moved into an apartment—that my mother secured for me—*knowing* I wanted to purchase a house. I didn't want to hurry through the process of figuring out what would work best for my family's needs. Staying in the apartment for five months allowed me to settle in and breathe, give birth to my son, get used to living by myself (with children), and slowly look at houses.

Those other little things that pop up will seem so insignificant that you'll be pissed you're being asked to deal with them. How *dare* I have a college final a week after my husband dies? How *dare* I have a dental appointment right now? How *dare* I have a pre-cancerous mole I need to have removed twelve days after I've buried my best friend?

All three of those examples were ones I dealt with within three weeks of my husband's death. Yours will be different. Perhaps you'll have to give a presentation at work, or fire a caregiver. Sometimes it just can't be postponed and you muddle through it as best as you can.

GIFTING. You'll be approached by family and friends asking for something to help them remember your loved one. A shirt. A picture. A lunch box. Whatever. Others are grieving, too. And sometimes the request won't come out so well. It might feel greedy to you, or insincere. Or maybe you'll just panic at the thought of giving something away that was your beloved's. Most likely you'll have a heart-felt request for some small to- ken, and they'll make it clear that you needn't bother with it until you are ready.

I, personally, gifted out Army pins, clothes, cuts of cloth (when more than one person wanted the same favorite flannel shirt), a Boston Bruins coat, and the head of a hockey stick.

YOU'LL HAVE VISITORS. But don't feel you have to entertain. Let them do for you. Ask for help, if you can. Otherwise, just let them be in the same room with you. They want to be helpful and they might not know how, so let them sit with you and not talk, or let them cry with you. Both can be cathartic.

At Home and Work

EMPLOYMENT/PAPERWORK. When I decided to quit my job after Rob died, my boss was genuinely confused. She thought it was best to keep busy when grieving. And so it is, for some. But truth be told, I *was* busy. So busy. At home I had a toddler, a pregnancy, doctor's appointments, calling creditors to cancel credit cards, and applying for death benefits from the Social Security office, the V.A., and my husband's place of business. I needed to get his things from work, I needed to invest the life insurance money I fortunately received, and I needed to sleep and grieve. It was all exhausting. I didn't have the time or energy for a job.

Unfortunately, some grieving spouses don't have this luxury, and some, I'm sorry to say, need to now get two jobs to fill the gap. If this is the case for you, *please*, seek as much assistance as possible from government programs, family, and friends. Again, you don't have to do this alone. It's best for all if you don't.

RELIGION/SPIRITUALITY. There is a great deal of variety here, and so much room for exploration. Some find refuge and com- fort in their church or religion; some lose their faith and leave it. As time passes, you might find yourself wanting to explore or practice a different religion or spiritual way of life. If you do, this is normal, too. After all, we are not the same as we were before our tragedy. The religion of my childhood couldn't serve me after my husband's death, so I explored other beliefs and found the right avenue for myself.

Some might feel threatened by your exploration, but this is your grief journey—a personal and private matter for you.

Don't let others bully you in, or out, of what you feel is right for you at this horrible time in your life. You are in charge. Even if it doesn't feel like it.

TELLING THE CHILDREN. This was terrifying for me. And it's tricky. It depends greatly on the age of the child. Different age groups have different cognitive abilities and needs, and require different communication from us. You must be careful what you say. Children are very literal-minded.

You don't want to say that the deceased love one is sleeping, because the child will continue to wait for them to wake up, or worse, not want to go to sleep themselves for fear of never waking up again.

And what if you say they've gone to heaven, and then they want to die so they can go to heaven, too? I was so worried about saying the wrong thing to my two-year-old daughter and scarring her for life. How do you tell your toddler that her daddy is dead?

Ultimately, I think you have to listen to your gut and then run it by someone else first. Talk to people who are familiar with this. Consult a counselor, a grieving expert, or other parents that are widows, or widowers.

This is how I did it:

I used Debi Gliori's picture book *No Matter What*. There is a passage that talks about love being like the stars that are far, far away. That the stars are still there even when you can't see them. I told my daughter that Daddy was far, far away like the stars, and that he couldn't come home, but that he'd love us forever—no matter what.

WHEN THE KIDS ARE GRIEVING. Of course my *unborn son* wouldn't grieve the loss of someone he didn't even know. It turns out though, that (later) kids in this situation sometimes *do*—grieve the loss of never having met a person they are so intimately connected with. Also, sometimes wee small ones just pick up on our sadness and grief, and will act out their own response to that.

I thought my daughter would be too young to remember her father and therefore wouldn't have the pain associated with grief, but about a year after Rob's death, she started saying she missed him. This was especially challenging for me because I was just hitting the 'Moving-on' stage and I was afraid that her outward mourning would set me back. I asked a therapist at that time if she thought my daughter needed counseling.

"No. Missing him is an appropriate behavior."

At three years old, she must have reached the cognitive ability to process out loud and talk about him. When she'd say, "I miss Daddy," I'd say, "Me, too," and she'd hug me and then be off to her next thing. That's all she wanted—a few extra minutes to say what she was feeling, and to be acknowledged for it. Perhaps that's all any of us want.

If your children are older, nine or twelve, say, then family counseling might be an excellent choice. There are many websites and other resources that outline (by age) what we can do to support our grieving children, such as answering questions clearly and honestly, and avoiding phrases like: "God took him," "He's gone to a better place,' or "She's sleeping in death now".

Reaching Out

WRITE IT DOWN/JOURNALING. I HAVE ALWAYS been a journal- er. But now I found it imperative. I needed to capture every memory I could think of and write it down. For me, for my children. And writing helped me organize my thoughts and feelings. Here are some other things that journaling can offer: a place to pour out the sorrow and venom, to remember, and to worry. And it was a place to recall the special moments that perhaps I'd taken for granted before, but was now so grateful that they'd happened.

I wrote every day. Several times a day. Sometimes I wrote letters: to my late husband, to my daughter, to my unborn child, to God, or to my angels/spirits/guides. Sometimes I had conversations in my journals. Mostly I just wrote about my emotional state. Getting fears and anxieties out of my head and on to paper was most therapeutic. Something about using my hands and processing feelings at the same time.

Journal writing was a lifeline for me—perhaps because I was a *Blended* griever. (See below in "Grieving Types.")

FINDING A MENTOR OR SUPPORT SYSTEM. You may feel that you already have a support system with your family and friends, and if you do, I'm so happy for you. You may feel that you don't need or want a counselor, or a support group. And you may be absolutely right in that.

Or you might not be.

I tried a couple of different things. I ate dinner at my sister-in-law's house so I didn't need to be alone on weekday nights; I visited my friends on the weekends when they were home from work; and I attended a grief support group a couple of times.

My friends were helpful, the support group wasn't. *For me.*

I want to stress that I think support groups are great. And I sort-of wish I'd continued going, or gone later, but with only three months between me and the death, I just didn't want to talk to a room full of strangers. And honestly, it didn't occur to me to find a counselor. But I *did* need something.

I found my something quite serendipitously. She was on a bulletin board. In the form of a brochure on stress-relieving meditation. She was a certified bereavement facilitator whose baby girl had died. This woman became part of my tribe.

I started seeing her once a week, and that was where my healing really began.

So don't immediately discount a third party mentor or support group. They really can do wonders for you. And if you try it and you don't feel a connection to your new therapist or grief support group, try another one. And maybe one more.

However, it is important to note that some people are not emotional grievers. They don't feel comfortable talking their feelings out. Maybe you are one of these. Perhaps you'd rather plant a flower garden in memory of your loved one, or paint a fence. If you are an active griever—someone that needs to do something physically to work through grief—these can be ways to process your emotions.

Every expression of grief is the right one. One book that made this so clear to me was *I'm Grieving As Fast As I Can* by Linda Feinberg. There are hundreds of accounts from young widows and widowers in such varied circumstances that they had to all grieve in different ways. Read it. You might just feel better. There are hundreds of accounts from young widows and widowers in such varied circumstances that they *had* to all grieve in different ways.

GRIEVING TYPES. In Dr. Kenneth Doka's book, *Disenfranchised Grief*, he describes four types of grievers: Intuitive, Instrumental, Blended, Dissonant.

Intuitive types are the ones with the outward emotions. They cry, feel exhausted and anxious, and/or have bouts of confusion.

Instrumental grievers are the ones compelled to Do Do Do. They don't particularly care for sharing their feelings and often just want to hurry up and "get better," as if grieving were an illness. These types of grievers could write letters, or train for a marathon to raise money for an organization that researches the type of disease that claimed their loved one. Perhaps they start a foundation. Or make a memory book.

Blended ones are—you guessed it—a combination of both. (And why I think journaling worked so great for me. I got to talk about my emotions...with my hands!)

Lastly, *dissonant* grievers are in conflict with their grieving style. Maybe they *want* to cry openly and tell their story but they are in a community or culture that frowns on it, so they hold it in. We sometimes see this in men in North America, and I've been told that the only safe place to cry in Asian countries is in a movie theater. Or the opposite: dissonant grievers might not be crying and feel like they should—feeling like they're being judged for not reacting properly to the death.

There is no one right way to grieve. Knowing what kind of griever you are may help you find some relief.

TELLING EVERYONE ELSE. Somehow all my family just seemed to *know* about Rob's death. I didn't have to tell anyone except my mom. Other than that, it took me *months* to tell anyone else. Running into marginal acquaintances or colleagues, or strangers at the YMCA or grocery store, didn't elicit any need on my part to randomly share my story with them. Three months after the fact, I did telephone our best man. I said what I had to say and hung up as fast as I could. I felt he should know, but I didn't feel comfortable chit-chatting with him about it afterwards. And that's okay.

You can do either. Or neither. If you want someone to know that a death has occurred, but you don't feel like handling it yourself, there is no shame in requesting assistance. The best approach is the direct one: "I think Bryan should know. Will you call and tell him? I'm just not up to it." People want to help.

LEARNING NEW THINGS. Without the expected companionship you are used to, you may find yourself with some extra time on your hands. Or maybe you feel busy, but your curiosity has returned. You might start reading books about reincarnation and jet fighter pilots, or take classes in permaculture design.

I was relieved when I started showing signs like these. One of my fears was that I'd never regain a zest for life. When I started reading again, I knew I was safe from that.

Carrying On

FINDING NEW FRIENDS AND LETTING GO OF OLD ONES. As if we didn't already have enough trauma in our lives right now, relationships with friends can change, too. Sometimes they can't be there for you during this time. Don't take it personally. And don't write them off. They're just grieving at a different rate than you are, or in a different way.

Grief changes relationships. It's unavoidable. Before the death, your friends related to you as a couple; now they don't. You definitely can lose your sense of self during this time. *(Who am I now without my partner?)* You will learn a lot about people through this process. Most of all, yourself.

Often other friends will step in when you least expect it to fill the void. Any desire to readjust who your friends are, and who you spend your time with, indicates a newfound inner strength. And that is always a cause for celebration.

C.A.M. CARE. Complementary Alternative Medicine is a way to nurture and take care of yourself. If your pocketbook allows it, try to receive some sort of preventative alternative therapy that brings you peace or pleasure once a week. And then adjust accordingly.

CAM refers to things like: acupuncture, Reiki, massage, emotional processing techniques, or other energy or body work. These are both helpful and healthful to you—physically, energetically, mentally, and emotionally. But CAM also includes other things that you can do to support yourself. Maybe that would be: a new bouquet of flowers for the kitchen table, a pedicure, or a month's supply of vitamins and supplements to keep your strength up. A writing retreat to France's cafes and bridges? Yes, please. Emotional R&R for sure.

More traditional care methods might be: lighting a candle at church every week, spending more time with relatives and friends, or quiet time in your garden or a favorite park.

My combination of CAM care was to receive relaxation massages every three weeks, get a pedicure once a month, and learning how to do Reiki on myself. I also promised myself an ocean cruise as soon as my baby was a year old. Which I took.

FEAR. I was always scared after Rob died. I spent months of worry about: physical safety *(Who would save me if someone broke into the house at night?)*, spiritual safety *(unreasonable fear of evil spirits attacking me)*, financial safety *(What if I made a bad investment?)*, and the constant fear of something happen- ing to my children or to myself—either going through another death, or leaving my children orphans.

Fear is normal, too. Try a visualization exercise of meeting Fear and seeing what it looks like. Talk to Fear. Whose face does it have? What does Fear gain by being in your life? What do you gain? Have a conversation. Sometimes that's all that needs to happen to get clarity. If it's too much, talk to someone.

Other more practical things you can do to alleviate some of your fears might be: getting AAA for roadside assistance in case of break-downs on dark nights; writing a will—with godparents for your children; adding a security system to your home; getting a dog.

And Beyond

THE FIRSTS. The first birthday without their dad. The first Halloween. The first Thanksgiving. The first Christmas. A bumpy ride for sure, but here's what helps:

- (1) Have a plan for the day. There will be less stress if you know what to expect from the event, and what part you are playing that day. For instance, "I will show up on time with my special baked beans, stay for two hours, and then leave. While I'm there I will play two card games and eat dinner."
- (2) Acknowledge that there's someone missing, and that it's weird and sad, and then carry on with the holiday anyway. This can be as simple as raising a glass before a special family meal and saying, "I just want to say that it's really terrible that Rob isn't with us today, but that I'm so thankful that you all are."
- (3) Mark the event somehow. Create a ritual. Sing happy birthday to the one that's died. Journal about the day without them. Make a photo album

of all the pictures you have of your loved one and give a copy to close family members.

ONE YEAR ANNIVERSARY. This is a doozy. The biggest of all the Firsts. As it happened, I was in the very best place for myself (geographically and socially) when the one year anniversary of Rob's death occurred. I was traveling to see family. This gave me a physical action with which to keep myself busy—travel- ing with very small children is a special kind of busy—*and* the opportunity to take some private time to acknowledge what day it was. I did this with journaling. After a day with my family, I carved out some time to sit in the backyard and journal. I lit candles and stayed outside until—one by one—the flames all went out.

STARTING AFRESH. This will happen at different times for *every- one*. There is no one right time to be "over" it. The reality is that you are never over it. There will probably always be soft longings, *what ifs*, or *if onlys* that can remain. But, *dang!* our society sure wants it that way. We only get three days of bereavement leave from work (and that's only if you are directly related to the deceased—my mother had to use vacation days to visit me, and my brothers-in-law only had one day off). We are often told we are "doing well" if we aren't showing any emotion. If we confess how horrible we actually feel inside, people are con- fused. "But I thought you were feeling better." As if grief were something to hurry up and get over.

Believe me. Most grieving people don't want to wallow in grief. It hurts. It makes you feel stupid, slow. You don't fit in anymore. Nothing makes sense anymore. If grieving were something we could just hurry up and get over with, we'd totally do it.

That being said, sometimes it does just feel like it's time to move on. Usually this is done in small steps. Perhaps you stop visiting the grave so often; maybe you finally scatter the ashes. Or you take off your wedding rings, and throw away his toothbrush.

Or maybe you move to a new state, like I did. (Though I'm not advising this, especially if you have no family or support there.) This *can* be rejuvenating. But just know that the grief will follow you. It may be less intense, or maybe it'll come out full force. Grief comes and goes as it wants to, as you are able to process it. And that's normal, too.

Around this time you might feel ready to start dating again. Or not. It's totally up to you. Some re-marry within the year; some never marry again. Any version of starting afresh is right and true, as long as you are checking in with yourself and listening to your voice instead of to the multitude of well mean- ing others.

GRIEF ISN'T ALL THAT EXCITING. Some might think otherwise. And parts of it sure are intense, but other parts of it are just like regular life. You need to take out the trash, so you do. You need to enroll your daughter in pre-school, so you do. Grieving all the while.

Grief hits you at mundane moments. While driving to the mountain to go snowshoeing for the first time—true story—or when seeing his favorite toothpaste at the store, or smelling his aftershave on your dad. Another true story. And grief is often a long drawn out general malaise-y feeling, rather than constant tears. Sometimes it's just numbness and forgetting why you were in a room.

CONTINUING CARE—EVEN A YEAR LATER. When I was first widowed, I looked around for someone to tell me how long it would take me to get through the grief process. *(Ha!)* I find that laughable now, but then I was totally serious. I gave it a good year. I thought that should handle it. But when a year had passed, and I was still feeling restless and unsettled and lonely and sad—despite "moving on" and starting school again and processing all that I thought I needed to process—I got irritated. I was tired of grieving; it was just so boring. Feeling depressed and miserable all the time just gets lame and uninspiring.

Some of what helped me over the restless boring part was still finding time for things that took me out of my headspace. Pedicures, a pottery class, massages, and jogging. Goals helped, too. I signed up for a marathon. Training and school work gave me something to do. And getting a roommate kept me social and prevented total isolation even if I was just at home in my pajamas. I also got to know the neighbors a little bit. And I started dating. Which was momentous.

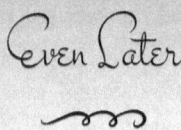

Even Later

DATING AGAIN. ALL I CAN REALLY SAY ABOUT THIS with any certainty is: It's personal. Here are some issues that might happen and need to be dealt with:

Someone thinks you are starting too soon, or shouldn't be doing it at all. Do it if you want to. And don't let anyone make you feel like it's too soon, or too late. I moved away so that his family didn't have to watch me go through the process. Sounds a tad drastic, and wasn't the only reason I moved. As I said before, I had support from other family members where I moved, so it wasn't as out of the blue as it may seem. It just so happened that the idea of dating other men while my late husband's family looked on was one of the things I considered when deciding whether to move, or not.

If you do start dating another, you might feel like you are betraying your late spouse. Totally normal. It took me a long time to come to terms with this one. But maybe it won't be an issue for someone else. My mother-in-law loves to say, "Everybody's different."

What to say to your children. Think age-appropriate conversations and explanations. Having "sleep-overs with your friend" might work for your three-year-old, but probably you'll have to have a longer discussion with your twelve-year-old. Some par- ents discuss everything with their children, others don't. Both are right. This is a parenting matter, as much as a personal matter. That means that *you* get to decide what's right for you and your children. Not your aunt or cousin. *You are the parent.*

PARENTING SIDE NOTE. I hereby give you permission to parent your children the best way you can with the circumstances you now live in.

For months I felt like a terrible mother for considering a babysitter for my kids. Our parenting plan (Rob's and mine) consisted of never having anyone watch our kids except a family member or really close friend.

My mother kindly set me straight and said, "You can't hold yourself accountable for keeping that rule you made back then. The circumstances were different. You don't have 70 aunts, uncles, and cousins to watch your kids anymore. You moved. You just do the best you can *now.*"

FOUR YEARS LATER. At this point, I felt I could safely say I was done grieving. I was in a long-term relationship; I'd become a licensed massage therapist; I'd kept up with my writing. My children were thriving; we had a puppy. But I was mad. Mad that Rob had died, mad that I didn't get to do the things we'd planned to do together, and mad that I'd had to go through the last four years. And I still missed him. I still wished he was alive and that we were together.

I realized in the end that this was okay. It was okay to love both my late husband, and the man I was with. It wasn't a betrayal.

But that was my path. Yours may look different, or take you to a separate place all together.

NEW BAGGAGE. These will come and go. Though some may stay forever. They could be things that show up years later. May- be you see how they are connected to your tragedy but it was weird that they didn't show up right away.

My new baggage includes: worrying about people who don't sleep enough, worrying about people driving when they are tired, having a twinge of fear of someone else driving my kids around town, my kids being out of town without me, being afraid of crashing my car when I drive in Massachusetts, having nightmares about my kids dying.

Mostly I don't dwell on these fears. I chalk them up as new *idiosyncrasies*.

GRIEF SHADOWS. Grief is cyclical. Not linear. It doesn't actually go away, like something you cross off on a checklist. This thought used to terrify me—that there would be this ever- present cloud hanging over my fragile state of mind, and that I would snap at any moment. But it's not like that at all. It's more like putting your hands in your pockets on a cold day and finding a leftover object. *"Oh, there's my lip balm."*

My grief shadows are: pear trees, Camel cigarettes, yellow rocks, seeing someone that resembles Rob, and a certain kind of giggle.

They don't make me sad. They evoke memories. Good ones, sad ones, poignant ones. They don't identify me, but they are a part of who I am now—part of the new me.

About the Author

I hope you found this booklet helpful. I wish you peace during your grief journey and in finding your new self. If you want to hear more about my story, pick up a copy of *Smell the Blue Sky: Young, Pregnant, and Widowed* wherever online books are sold.

Valerie Ihsan is the author of You Can't Dance a Lie: A Memoir of Stepping into My Truth (March 2023); <u>The Scent of Apple Tea;</u> and <u>Smell the Blue Sky: Young, Pregnant, and Widowed</u>, **winner of a B.R.A.G. Medallion for Top Indie-Published Books**. She co-chaired the Eugene Chapter of Willamette Writers for ten years; and podcasts, coaches, and edits for authors. She's served in the United States Army, owns land in Costa Rica, and lives with her husband and three dogs in Springfield, Oregon. She loves chocolate, cheese, and dogs.

Smell the Blue Sky: Young, Pregnant, and Widowed

Chapter One

> "We've only been apart for about two hours now and I miss the hell out of you. I feel so comfortable with you. I haven't been this happy in a long time..."
> ~*Rob; love letter excerpt*

A DOORBELL RINGS THROUGH FUZZY SLEEP AND I look at the clock. 1:00 a.m. *Rob?* I flip back the covers and pull on Rob's navy robe. It's closer than mine. I rush down the green shag carpeted hall to the door – sleep still sticking to my eyes. Rob's mom, Fernanda, beats me there. She unbolts the door and we see Rob standing on the other side. *What's he doing here?* He's supposed to be on Cape Cod doing his Annual Training for the National Guard.

He steps through the white screen door that always slams too hard and hugs his mom. The humid summer night clings to his clothes.

"*Aiy!* Why are you here?" Fernanda says.

"I'm here to see you. Just for a little bit, then I need to get back. I missed you." A big smile. White teeth against his dark "*Portagee*" skin, black hair, and sooty lashes.

They embrace warmly. I smile at Rob over Fernanda's shoulder. He smiles back and his eyes speak of tenderness. Fernanda gets one more smooch and pads downstairs to her section of the house. Her feet on the stairs make happy sounds.

Rob and I retire to the bathroom. It's our favorite place to talk. Many heartfelt confessions have been revealed at two or three in the morning in that blue and white tiled bathroom. The noisy and annoying overhead fan is perfect for private conversations. Even though we have our own living space, privacy is still an issue while we live with Rob's mom.

So that's where I tell him that after *eight months of trying*, we finally have Baby Number Two on the way. Our toddler will get her sibling. Rob bounces up and down on the balls of his feet – his knees rigid – and giggles. We hug and cry with relief, excitement and anticipation.

IN THE KITCHEN, ROB YAWNS. I HAND HIM A TRAVEL mug for his drive back in our silver Explorer.

"Why go now? It's almost two in the morning. Just stay the night and drive back to the base in a few hours. Sleep now." I pull at his jacket and plead. A forty-five minute visit in the middle of the night – just because – isn't as satisfying as you'd think. He still has a week left of his training.

"I can't." He smiles knowingly. "I'd never wake up in time for formation."

I droop. He's right. We walk to the door and hug again.

"Drive safe."

"Always," he says. He looks down at me from his additional five inches.

"I love you, " I say.

He walks through the door and as I close it behind him a song from *Alabama,* unbidden, comes to mind. I sway down the dark hall, singing about angels working among us during dark hours of the soul, and climb back in bed smiling. Rob knows. We're pregnant. And our beautiful baby girl is sleeping beside our bed in the crib. Life is wonderful.

THE FIVE A.M. KNOCK AT THE DOOR SENDS fingernails of dread scratching the blackboard of my mind. Funny how the one a.m. doorbell didn't scare me but the five a.m. knock does. I stumble to the window and see a flashlight beam shining in the dark. Three uniforms appear from the shadows; stiff navy blue fabric hold the men rigid. It is Thursday, August 17, 2000.

"Mrs. Gomes-Pereira?"

"Yes," I say. My lips feel dry; I clutch Rob's robe tighter around me.

"May we come in?"

"Who is it?" Fernanda's voice asks from out of the darkness. She had followed me into the parlor. "Who's here?" she demands in a Portuguese accent.

I feel dazed. *Rob*. I grapple with the screen door lock.

Nothing is said. The silence shouts at me and I watch the somber faces file into the dining room. The face in the back closes the door. The one in front, a mustached man of fifty, holds up a scrap of paper.

"Does Robert Gomes-Pereira live here?"

"Yes," I whisper. My legs betray me and I drop onto the computer chair.

"I don't know how to tell you this, ma'am, but there's been an accident and he didn't make it."

My breath raggles to a stop. I look at each of the three Massachusetts state troopers one at a time. My brain can't take these words and make sense of them. They just float and roll in the waves like soggy driftwood. Through blurry eyes I see Fernanda bend over and stumble, like Grief punched her in the stomach.

"My poor boy. *Meu filho!*" Fernanda wails. She lunges at the telephone receiver and stops. Horror.

"The number! What's the number? Why can't I ... I don't remember ..."

I know she means Gerry's, of course. I recite my sister-in-law's phone number and look over at the green pseudo-suede parlor sofa and the "throne" chair that Rob will never inherit from his mom.

"Do you want us to stay until someone gets here for you?" The mustached trooper steps forward, the forgotten scrap of paper still in his hand.

"My sister-in-law is coming." I see the troopers getting restless, wanting to leave this suffocating haze of grief before them, but I want to know what happened. The two younger men shift their hats and clear their throats.

The man with the mustache is talking again. I look into his apologetic eyes and struggle to understand. He's saying something about the accident. I try to listen but a tiny green fuzz nestled between his shirt collar and neck distracts me.

"It appears he fell asleep driving. He hit an exit signpost on Route 25."

A wave rises from my stomach to my throat. I swallow and shut my eyes. No tears come, but I hear crying. It isn't me; it's Aubrey. I hurry to our bedroom and lift her out of the crib, grateful to escape the nothingness in the parlor.

Aubrey's thick toddler hair is damp from the sweaty room but despite the humidity she clings to me as if scared. Another clunk in my throat. *Can she know already?*

Back in the parlor, Fernanda sobs something and reaches for Aubrey, but she must be frightened of all the tears and sounds coming from her beloved *Vavo*, because Aubrey grasps instead to me. And grateful, I bury my nose deep in her hair and croon softly in her ear until the uniformed faces leave.

STILL WEARING ROB'S ROBE, I STARE AT NOTHING. Somewhere in the back a TV sings inappropriately cheery songs to occupy the innocent Aubrey. Fernanda shuffles back and forth moaning and praying under her breath. I look at the floor. *I have to call my mom.* It's time. I find myself back in my bedroom, a haven of sorts – though you wouldn't think so anymore. I blink at the phone. Sandpaper eyes. My right index finger dials the number. I stare at its ragged cuticle.

This isn't real, I promise myself. The answering machine picks up. It's 2:30 a.m. in Oregon. Should I leave a message? What would I say? *'Hi Mom, Call me back. Rob's dead?'*

I push my fingers into my eyes and take a deep breath.

"Mom? It's Valerie. Are you awake? Wake up. I need to talk to you." I wait, holding my breath, hiding in the dark of our bedroom.

"Hello? Valerie? I couldn't find the phone ..."

"Mom!" I'm so relieved that she's truly there that the word gushes out. "Mom. Rob died this morning -- in a car accident." My throat swells and it feels like something is squishing my esophagus. Darkness burns the edges of my mind, curling them like charred paper. I start to shake and finally a few tears come. But not nearly enough to dislodge the huge boulder pressing at my lungs.

My mom thrives in a crisis. I know this. All my life I've seen her take on a billion tasks at a time and succeed at everything she does. A daunting example to follow, sure, but I know that when I call her, she will know exactly what to do.

I don't really hear anything she says on the phone. Only, "I'll be there. I'll figure it out and call you back in a few hours. I love you."

I drift downstairs and sit on the floor, aching for Aubrey, so beautiful, so oblivious. I ache for Rob, too. *Is he really gone? What am I going to do now?*

I want to grow old with Rob.

We had just received our passports in the mail. We planned to go to France and Germany in the Spring. A sour feeling rises within me, tainting my cells and pores with stink. The European family trip is only one of many dreams that he and I will never realize. Our family is broken.

Where will I go now? Who will I belong to? Where will I fit in?

A door slamming and a flurry of steps interrupt my thoughts. I force my head to turn and I get up from the floor where I'm slumped.

"Mom! Valerie!" *Thud, thud, thud* down the stairs – racing to get to us. Rob's two sisters, Gerry and Lena, burst around the corner. I raise my arms to them and we embrace and lean into each other, seeking comfort. We weep and snuffle and choke, snot and tears smearing together.

And then they turn to their mother.

Gerry is the oldest. She wears fun plastic glasses in trendy styles and hands me buckets of quarters when we visit casino slot machines on special occasions. She blinks when she talks and has a quiet but sing-songy voice. It's pretty fast, too – her voice. And she laughs when she talks. Her laugh is loud and tinkly, like wind-chimes. I love it.

Lena is the middle child. *Was.* Her and Rob, as children, were always together – sought comfort from each other. Were buddies. Lena is self-deprecating and can always make me smile. She smokes – something else she shared with Rob. Me too, actually, until 10 p.m. last night when I found out I was pregnant. No more smoking now though. Not with this little one inside me. I touch my belly with a frantic, yet smoothing, gesture. Lena wears sensible shoes and swimsuits that cover everything up and never lets anyone in her apartment. Not even her mom. I've never seen it. She laughs when she talks, too.

I wonder when any of us will do that again – laugh.

Over the next couple of hours, more family arrives to share condolences and grief. Some bring me comfort and strength where I have none. Some come in an outpouring of grief and I splash into the waves and cry, too. I feel small relief from these tears, though. They are never enough.

My crying strikes me as too dainty, or polite. I want to sob and thrash, to keen and wail. I feel weird and unsettled by it. I suppose I must be in shock, but then I wouldn't *know* I was in shock, would I? Like a crazy person doesn't know he's crazy.

I sit in a folding chair next to the phone downstairs. I'm waiting for State Trooper Brito to call me back and give me any more information about the accident. He found Rob. I'm waiting for the morgue to call me back, too, so we can tell them where to send the body.

Actually, I don't really know why I'm sitting here. I'm just waiting. Waiting to know what to do. Waiting to feel something and conversely to not feel anything. I just stare at the floor and at the phone cord twisting down long, past the red Formica countertops.

Two or three people mill around the kitchen and the

boiler room where Fernanda hangs up our clothes to dry in the winter – the ones she doesn't put in the dryer. The rest of the basement room is ringed by family members sitting haggard in chairs. Our life without Rob has barely begun and we already look hollow.

The boiler room beckons.

Maybe someone is hiding in there now. Hiding from the rest of the faces, crying.

When Lena and Gerry first came over, before the rest of the family knew, Lena disappeared out in the backyard for awhile. I imagine what she must've done out there. Pacing in the dewy grass, her hands in fists, punching the air with them and beating her knees and sobbing and then wilting down to the back step and hugging her knees to her chest, trembling, rocking, and smoking a cigarette.

I wish I had the energy to be out there doing the same thing instead of sitting by this phone. But I only seem to be able to sit, with my hands in my lap, or holding my head up. With barely the awareness to breathe. Sometimes I even forget to do that and a cavernous sigh rushes out up from my knees. And then I forget to do it again until the next rush.

It hasn't even been three hours since I've heard of his death – maybe eight since I've seen him last – but I already miss him.

I miss how his eyes half shut and he looks at me underneath his lashes. I miss the sound of his giggle when he gets shy or nervous.

A sad smile tries to lift the corners of my mouth. He giggles like that when I tickle him, too. Or when we have sex. Sometimes he gets all vampire-ish. His eyes flash and sparkle and he gets this evil grin on his face, and then he growls at me. I miss that already, too.

I love it when his eyes fill up with love – sometimes he says, "I love you," and other times he swallows it back. When I see that, my heart melts and I know I'm the most important person in the world.

All my organs sink lower into my body and my blood congeals. *I'm no longer that important person anymore.* Will I ever be? It dawns on me that all those things I miss about Rob, are now things that I *missed* about him. Because he no longer *is,* but *was.* He's now in the past tense. My vision narrows, a black circle compressing my corneas, and I collapse into myself.

Portuguese families are big. They are full of noisy, overbearing, loving and helpful people. I rely on this aid now and lean into it. My favorite of Rob's extended family is his godfather and uncle, Louie. He's here now, wandering from room to room – benevolence and compassion and pain exuding from every neuron. He is calm and charming with twinkling blue eyes. They always hold a joke in them. He reminds me a little of my own uncle.

I was welcomed by all of Rob's family when we moved to Massachusetts after our Military Occupational Skill (MOS) training, but I felt it soonest with Louie. It enveloped me and I got the feeling that no matter what I'd ever do, I'd be welcomed and loved in his house.

He's religious, but more open-minded than I expected. He's firm, but loving. And, for a while, he took Rob into his home to live when Rob was an obnoxious, at-risk teenager playing around with drugs and alcohol. Fernanda thought he'd be safer under Louie's firm hand for a bit. So Louie is alright by me.

And when he steps in to handle some of the phone calls and family affairs, I am relieved. No one has to ask him, he just does it. Especially when I take the call from Rob's unit looking for him.

In a voice that doesn't sound like me, I explain that he died that morning and the caller is so incredulous she asks me to repeat myself three times. Fed up, I shout in the phone, "He's dead!" That's when Louie steps up to finish the call. I rock in my seat and stare at the floor. I hear Louie's voice but don't know what he is saying.

Lena asks about food, knowing of my pregnancy, and a dry bagel materializes. Gerry offers to take Aubrey home with her to be with the cousins.

"She's so little that I'm worried all the somberness and tears might be frightening for her. But whatever you think best. Whatever you want, Valerie."

At first I say no. I want her warm, *live* body close by because Rob's is so clearly not. But an hour or so later I change my mind. It will be better, healthier, for Aubrey to not be here – to go to Gerry's instead.

I wonder how much Aubrey knows about what's going on? She sits on the floor, chatting delightfully to her toys -- but that only makes it sadder somehow because now I see Rob lying on the floor with her last Christmas, building towers and houses with her fat new Legos while she watches them grow bigger and taller – a red one clutched in her hands. Every once in a while, she hands him a Lego.

And months after that, Rob on the floor again -- this time in his shirt and tie from work – answering Aubrey as she toddles about the room pointing to objects and asking, "This? ... This? ... This?" She wants to know the names of everything and Rob's proud smile that day will forever be with me.

I wonder if Aubrey will remember it.

AFTER AUBREY AND MOST OF THE FAMILY LEAVES, I make my way to the shower. I know with certainty that now, alone, I will be able to cry those real tears. They will come, I know.

Rob was my soulmate. *There's that* was *again*. We both

knew it. Felt it. The day we met, we shared a pizza and conversation. The next week we started dating. Three months later we were married and exactly one year later, on our anniversary, our daughter was born. We were so closely linked in spirit we often thought the same thoughts, at the same time. Of course I will cry.

But alone in the dark, the real tears still do not come.

What am I going to do now? How am I going to live without you? I ask the wall. I feel no anger, only sorrow and emptiness. I feel as if I am perpetually holding my breath. *It doesn't matter how I live. I just have to. For Aubrey. For the new baby.*

Water pounds my skin and the shower mists blanket me, and even though I never pray any other time, here now in this shower I do. "Dear God, Whoever you are, please. Please give me strength and courage to make it through this day." I shudder to think what will follow 'this day'.

Dripping, I step over the side of the porcelain tub. Water soaks into the cotton bathmat. Reaching for a towel, I catch sight of a lone sunbeam shining through the slats of the blinds. It's a strong beam, bright and steady in the dark room.

Awed, I whisper, "Thank you, God. I know you're here." I dry off in silence and join the house of mourners with renewed strength. Still with heavy heart and full of sorrow, yes, but now with a quiet strength inside me. For the moment at least. But that's all I had asked for, strength and courage for the day.

Free Offer

Two Exclusive Essays

OH, THE WOES OF GROCERY shopping, and finding time to write in the summer.

Valerie battles with everyday tasks, like getting her kids to *stop with the video-gaming already!*, gardening, and making meaning in the mundane. **Download these irreverent, cheeky (and somehow still poignant) essays today.**